P9-CFD-617

A Classic Collection of
Golf Jokes
& Quotes

BOB PHILLIPS

HARVEST HOUSE PUBLISHERS

Eugene, Oregon 97402

Cover by Terry Dugan Design, Minneapolis, Minnesota

A CLASSIC COLLECTION OF GOLF JOKES AND QUOTES

Copyright © 2001 by Bob Phillips
Published by Harvest House Publishers
Eugene, Oregon 97402

ISBN 0-7369-0694-0

All rights reserved. No part of this publication may be reproduced, stored in a retrieval system, or transmitted in any form or by any means—electronic, mechanical, digital, photocopy, recording, or any other—except for brief quotations in printed reviews, without the prior permission of the publisher.

Printed in the United States of America.

01 02 03 04 05 06 07 08 09 10 / BP-MS / 10 9 8 7 6 5 4 3 2 1

Contents

Golf in
One Stroke

Only a remarkable man can live down a hole in one.

You play golf with your worst enemy—yourself.

Nothing improves a golfer's disposition like finding a better ball than he went looking for.

Even Samson couldn't break away from the links.

Many a man who doesn't play golf can't give it up.

Golf is a lot like business. You drive hard to get in the green and then wind up in the hole.

The difference between golf and tennis is that in tennis you want to kill the other player; in golf you just want to kill yourself.

Golf is an ideal hobby, but a ruinous disease.

Playing golf is easy. You just swing the club and say, "Oh, no...no!"

Golf is nothing but pool played out of doors.

In golf, the ball always lies poorly, and the player lies well.

On a public golf course, you hit a ball, and a public runs out and grabs it.

The secret of golf is to hit the ball hard, straight, and not too often.

Golf is the most popular way of beating around the bush.

Golf is flog spelled backward!

Golf has made more liars out of the American people than the income tax.

Golf is a game where everyone in front is too slow, and everyone behind is too fast.

There are three ways to improve your golf score: take lessons, practice often, or start cheating.

A golfer is a gardener digging up someone else's lawn.

A well-adjusted person is one who can play golf and bridge as if they were games.

If you think it's hard to meet new people, pick up the wrong golf ball.

A golf club is another name for a shovel.

Par is attained with a soft pencil and a softer conscience.

A handicapped golfer is one who plays with his boss.

When you're playing golf, nothing counts like your opponent.

You can judge a man by the golf score he keeps.

Golf is a lot of walking, broken up by disappointment and bad arithmetic.

The modern executive talks golf all morning in the office, and business all afternoon on the links.

A man who pushes a lawn mower and calls it work is the same man who pushes a golf cart and calls it recreation.

Spring is when the farmer and the golfer start their plowing together.

As soon as a businessman takes up golf, he becomes an executive.

All is fair in love and golf.

His friends call it madness, but he calls it golf.

Beating Around the Bush

And of course you know the one about the dentist who refused to make an appointment with a patient because of a busy afternoon.

"I've got 18 cavities to fill," he said as he picked up his golf bag and left his office.

I have a friend who needs psychological help. He treats golf as if it were a game!

While we waited to tee off on the fifteenth hole, a man in the foursome ahead drove three successive balls smack into the water.

In a fit of temper he picked up his golf bag and hurled it into the lake, then stamped off toward the clubhouse.

We weren't surprised to see him sheepishly return a few minutes later, roll up his pants, take off his shoes, and wade in after the clubs. It was what we'd expected.

But to our amazement, he fished out the bag, unzipped the pocket, took out his car keys, flung the clubs into the water again, and stalked off.

—LOUIS H. WILLIAMS

A historian says that a game something like golf was played in A.D. 1089. This game is played still.

When you putt well, you are a good putter. But when the other fellow is putting well, he has a good putter.

Pro: Your trouble is that you don't address
    the ball properly.
Novice: Well, I was polite to the darn thing
    as long as possible.

Man blames fate for other accidents, but
feels personally responsible when he makes
a hole in one.

First golfer: Two! I saw you take six
    strokes.
Second golfer: Four were to kill the rat-
    tlesnake.

A chap who played golf in a foursome with President Eisenhower at the Cherry Hills Club in Denver shanked an approach shot. To his horror, the errant pellet flew toward the President and hit him in the right rear pocket. The mortified player raced toward the Chief Executive, all apologies. "Mr. President," he exclaimed, "I hope you aren't hurt."

The President gingerly rubbed the place where the ball had hit.

"I carry my wallet back there," said Ike. "This is the first time I've been touched there without being hurt!"

—MAURIE LUXFORD, QUOTED BY ART ROSENBAUM

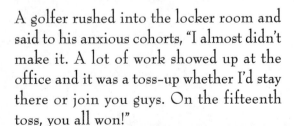

A golfer rushed into the locker room and said to his anxious cohorts, "I almost didn't make it. A lot of work showed up at the office and it was a toss-up whether I'd stay there or join you guys. On the fifteenth toss, you all won!"

A golfer was sitting in the den talking to a friend on the phone. "I am master of my home and I can play golf anytime I want to. Just hold the phone a minute while I find out if I want to."

A guy went into a sporting goods store to get some golf balls.

"Shall I wrap them up?" asked the clerk.

"No," said the man. "Just tee them off. I'll drive them home."

First friend: Why do you play golf?

Second friend: To aggravate myself!

Two men were searching frantically for almost an hour looking for their golf balls that went into the rough.

An elderly woman sitting on a bench was watching them. After quite a period of time she approached them and asked, "I don't want to bother you gentlemen, but would it be cheating if I were to tell you where the balls are?"

First golfer: I got some new golf clubs for my wife.
Second golfer: Gee, that's great! I wish I could make a trade like that!

A young man wanted his new girlfriend to learn to play golf. He was explaining the game to her. "The idea of the game," he said, "is to knock a ball into a hole with as few strokes as possible."

"Oh," she said demurely, "that sounds exciting. Sort of like basketball. And are you supposed to try to stop me?"

Golfer: What do you think would go well with my purple-and-green golf socks?
Wife: Hip boots.

A homeless person was curled up asleep underneath some shrubbery near the tee on a swank Palm Desert golf course. The club secretary and the pro were playing an early round together when they found the sleeping man. The club secretary woke him up with a swift kick. "Get up," he shouted. "You aren't supposed to sleep here."

"Who do you think you are," the bum asked, "waking me out of a comfortable nap?"

"I'm the club secretary and chairman of the membership committee," the man said. "That's who I am."

"Well," responded the homeless person, "all I can say is, that's a lousy way to try to get new members."

First golfer: Look at that foursome ahead of us. That's sure going to be a battle of wits.

Second golfer: What do you mean, it's going to be a battle of wits? How can a game of golf be a battle of wits?

First golfer: Look who's playing: Horowitz, Muscowitz, Shimkowitz and Lefkowitz.

One golfer, in a golf cart, to another: "Since I've straightened out my drives, I've been shooting this course consistently in less than two pints of gas!"

A duffer complained to his friend, "Don't ever play golf with Bob Martin. Yesterday, he wouldn't even concede a two-foot putt."

"Why fuss about it?" his friend asked.

"Because it cost me three strokes, that's why," said the first golfer.

Sign posted in British golf club in Africa: *If the ball comes to rest in dangerous proximity to a crocodile or a hippopotamus, another ball may be dropped.*

An irate man came rushing out of his home which faced the golf course. "Hey, there! Look what you did! You hooked your drive and the ball broke my big picture window. What are you going to do about it?"

The golfer looked at him earnestly and said, "I think I'll try a more relaxed grip and maybe hold my elbow in a little closer."

Average golfer: Forty around the chest, 38 around the waist, 96 around the course, nuisance around the house.

First golfer: What's the quickest way to beat my brother-in-law at golf?
Second golfer: Give him a book on how to play.

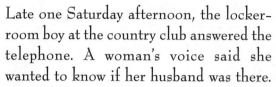

Late one Saturday afternoon, the locker-room boy at the country club answered the telephone. A woman's voice said she wanted to know if her husband was there.

"No, lady," he said. "He isn't here."

"How can you say he isn't there?" she asked. "I haven't even told you my name yet."

"It doesn't matter, lady," he said. "There ain't never anybody's husband here on Saturday afternoon."

George Washington never told a lie. Of course he never played golf or filed an income tax return either.

A behavioral scientist taught an ape to play golf. One day he tested his work on a real golf course. The ape teed off and hit the ball 400 yards on the fly. The ball landed two feet from the cup. The ape studied his position, then took another swing and hit the ball another 400 yards.

First golfer: I usually shoot in the low 90s.
Second golfer: Kinda hot to play golf.

On the completion of an irrigation project in India, the American engineer who had bossed the job was offered a tremendous sum of money as a bonus. When it was politely refused, the maharajah who had made the offer tried again, this time with a hatful of priceless gems. But the American still said no, explaining that the contract price was more than adequate for the work done. But still the potentate persisted, and the American finally relented to the point of agreeing to accept some token gift.

"I am a golf enthusiast," he said. "So if you want to give me something, I'd like very much to have three matched golf clubs."

Months went by. The American engineer had long since returned home and had all but forgotten the proposed gift. Then one day a cablegram arrived from the maharajah reading as follows: "Have finally been able to buy three golf clubs in your country. Sorry they don't quite match. Only two of them have swimming pools."

Overheard on the Green

Golf is a game where guts and blind devotion will always get you absolutely nothing but an ulcer.

—TOMMY BOLT

It matters not whether you win or lose; what matters is whether I win or lose.

—DARIN WEINBERG

Golf teaches success and failure. Neither lasts long.

—GLENN KUMMER

If there is any reward I treasure most, it is the way that the game of golf has responded to my inner drives, to the feeling we all have that—in those moments that are so profoundly a challenge to man himself—he has done his best. That—win or lose—nothing more could have been done.

—ARNOLD PALMER

You've just one problem. You stand too close to the ball—after you've hit it.

—SAM SNEAD

I asked my caddie for a sand wedge and he came back ten minutes later with a ham on rye.

—CHI CHI RODRIGUEZ

There are three ways of learning golf: by study, which is the most wearisome; by imitation, which is the most fallacious; and by experience, which is the most bitter.

—ROBERT BROWNING

I've thrown a few clubs in my day. In fact, I guess at one time or another I held distance records for every club in the bag.

—TOMMY BOLT

The secret's in the dirt. Dig it out like I did.

—BEN HOGAN

I'm in the woods so much I can tell you which plants are edible.

—LEE TREVINO

No one who ever had lessons would have a swing like mine.

—LEE TREVINO

Would you like to know the fastest way to take several strokes off of your game? Spend two hours in a bunker.

—GREG NORMAN

Golf appeals to the idiot in us, and the child. Just how childlike golfers become is proven by their frequent inability to count past five.

—JOHN UPDIKE

I used to play golf with a guy who cheated so badly that he once had a hole in one and wrote down zero on his scorecard.

—BOB BRUCE

The best advice I can offer for playing a ball out of water is—don't.

—TONY LEMA

I play in the low 80s. If it's any hotter than that, I don't play.

—JOE E. LEWIS

There's an old saying: If a man comes home with sand in his cuffs and cockleburs in his pants, don't ask him what he shot.

—Sam Snead

Golf is a game whose aim is to hit a very small ball into an even smaller hole, with weapons singularly ill designed for the purpose.

—Winston Churchill

There are long cleeks and short cleeks, driving cleeks, lofting cleeks, and putting cleeks; there are heavy irons and light irons, driving irons, lofting irons, and sand irons. There are mashies and niblicks. In this multitude of golf clubs there is wisdom—somewhere—but it can scarcely be that all of them are necessary.

—Horace Hutchinson

To find a man's true character, play golf with him.

—P. G. WODEHOUSE

The person I fear most in the last two rounds is myself.

—TOM WATSON

Never bet with anyone who has a deep tan, squinty eyes, and a one iron in his bag.

—DAVE MARR

If I can give you any advice, it's don't listen to any advice.

—BRUCE FLEISHER

There is no similarity between golf and putting; they are two different games—one is played in the air, and the other on the ground.

—BEN HOGAN

Putting allows the touchy golfer two to four opportunities to blow a gasket in the short space of two to 40 feet.

—TOMMY BOLT

Just tee it up and hit it, and when you find it, hit it again.

—DON JANUARY

Golf is the most human game of all. You have the same highs and lows—sometimes in the same round.

—LEE TREVINO

Golf is the cruelest game, because eventually it will drag you out in front of the whole school, take your lunch money, and slap you around.

—RICK REILLY

You know those two-foot downhill putts with a break? I'd rather see a rattlesnake.

—SAM SNEAD

The only shots you can be dead sure of are those you've had already.

—BYRON NELSON

I tried. I swung. I missed. I never tried again.

—ALEKSANDR SOLZHENITSYN

No one has as much luck around the greens as one who practices a lot.

—CHI CHI RODRIGUEZ

I've got a new idea. Try the fairway.

—BILL CLINTON

The toughest opponent of all is Old Man Par. He's a patient soul who never shoots a birdie and never incurs a bogey. He's a patient soul, Old Man Par. And if you would travel the long road with him, you must be patient, too.

—BOBBY JONES

That was the worst swing I ever heard.

—CHARLEY BOSWELL
CHAMPIONSHIP BLIND GOLFER

Reverse every natural instinct and do the opposite of what you are inclined to do, and you will probably come very close to having a perfect golf swing.

—BEN HOGAN

Caddie Stories

Golfer: You must be pooped from carrying
   my clubs so long.
Caddie: I'm not tired of carrying, but I'm
   sure tired of counting!

Golfer: Caddie, are you good at finding balls?
Caddie: Yes, sir!
Golfer: Well, go out and find one now and
   we'll start.

New golfer: I want to be a golfer in the
   worst way.

Caddie: You've already made it, sir!

A caddie is one of those little things that count; the worse the better.

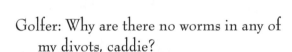

Golfer: Why are there no worms in any of my divots, caddie?
Caddie: They're probably all hiding under the ball, sir.

Golfer: How should I play this putt, caddie?
Caddie: Try to keep it low, sir.

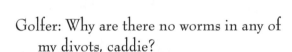

Golfer: Will this iron get me home, caddie?

Caddie: I can't say; I don't know where you live.

Judge: Do you understand the nature of an oath?

Boy: Do I? Ain't I your caddie?

After a round of 142, the golfer said to his caddie, "Am I the worst golfer you ever caddied for?"

The caddie said, "I'm not about to say that, but I've been in spots today I never knew were on the property."

A golfer and his caddie argued about which club to use on a short hole. Instead of the recommended number three iron, the golfer used his driver and hit a shot that sliced sharply to the right, hit a tree, bounced back across the green where it struck a rock and caromed—yes, you guessed it—right into the hole.

Amid whoops of joy, the happy golfer turned to the caddie and said, "See, I told you that was the right club."

Golfer: Caddie, guess you've gone around with worse golfers than me. (Brief pause.) Caddie, I said, I guess you've gone around with worse golfers than me.

Caddie: Heard you the first time, sir. Just mulling it over.

Golfer: Got a suggestion on my game, caddie?

Caddie: Yes, sir. Try laying off for 30 days.

Golfer: Then what?

Caddie: Then quit.

First golfer: What do you think I ought to leave for the caddie?

Second golfer: Your clubs!

Golfer: Well, caddie, I guess I'm about the worst golfer in the world.

Caddie: Oh no, sir, there are a lot worse than you, but they don't play.

Golfer: Caddie, when do I get to use the
     putter?
Caddie: Please, sir, sometime before dark.

Golfer: I'm certainly not playing my usual
     game.
Caddie: What game is that?

Golfer: How would you play that lie?
Caddie: Certainly under an assumed name,
     sir.

Golfer: You perhaps won't believe it, but I
     once did this hole in one.
Caddie: Stroke or day, sir?

Golfer: Notice any improvements in my
    game?
Caddie: Shined your clubs?

First golfer: Why are you using two caddies
    today?
Second golfer: Because my wife feels I
    don't spend enough time with my kids.

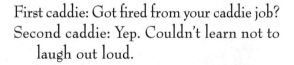

First caddie: Got fired from your caddie job?
Second caddie: Yep. Couldn't learn not to
    laugh out loud.

A golfer was having an awful day on the public links. Finally, on the eleventh green, he blew a six-inch putt. That did it. He cursed up a storm, threw the ball as far as he could, and then broke every club in his bag. Then he turned to his caddie and said, "I've got to quit."

"Quit golf?" asked the caddie.

"No, the priesthood," said the golfer.

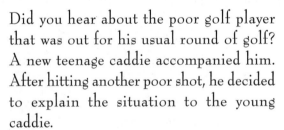

Did you hear about the poor golf player that was out for his usual round of golf? A new teenage caddie accompanied him. After hitting another poor shot, he decided to explain the situation to the young caddie.

"You see, I recently took up golf to practice self-control," he said.

"Really?" replied the teenager. "In that case, you should have become a caddie."

A golfer who had made a spectacularly bad shot and torn up a large piece of turf took the sod in his hand, and looking wildly about, asked: "What shall I do with this?"

"If I were you," said the caddie, "I'd take it home to practice on."

An American was playing golf in Scotland for the first time. He was having a terrible day. He was very unhappy about it and was complaining to his caddie.

"These are terrible links. The worst I have ever played."

"I'm sorry, sir," said the caddie. "But we are not playing on the links. You got off of them two hours ago."

Like most beginners, the golfer managed to hit one magnificent, long drive during the 18 holes. When the round was over, he couldn't stop boasting about that particular shot.

"Wasn't that drive marvelous?" he asked the caddie for the tenth time.

"Yes," was the reply. "It's a shame you can't have it stuffed!"

Golfer: If you laugh at me again, I'll knock your block off.

Caddie: Haw, haw; you wouldn't even know what club to use.

Well Putt

A group of golfers were telling tall stories. At last came a veteran's turn.

"Well," he said, "I once drove a ball, accidentally of course, through a cottage window. The ball knocked over an oil lamp and the place caught on fire."

"What did you do?" asked his friends.

"Oh," said the veteran, "I immediately teed another ball, took careful aim, and hit the fire alarm on Main Street. That brought out the fire engine before any major damage was done."

They call someone who has played in the sand all day—Lawrence of Arabia.

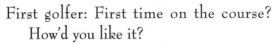

First golfer: First time on the course?
    How'd you like it?
Second golfer: Not bad. Shot a 68.
First golfer: Pretty good! Playing tomorrow?
Second golfer: Yep. Tomorrow I'm going
    after the second hole.

First golfer: There's a new dictionary of
    golfing terms just out.
Second golfer: Well, if it's complete it will
    be banned.

You can tell a boss and the employee. The
employee is the one who makes a hole in
one and says, "Oops!"

Did you hear about the schoolteacher who was playing golf for the first time?
"Is the word spelled P-U-T-T or P-U-T?" she asked the golf pro.

"P-U-T-T is correct," he responded. "P-U-T means to place something where you want it. P-U-T-T means to make a vain attempt to do the same thing."

It is the golf season so I thought I'd give you some advice: If you break 100, watch your golf. If you break 80—watch your business.

Duffers

The club duffer cornered the club pro at the bar one afternoon. "Say, how can I cut down my strokes?"

"Take up painting!"

A duffer is one who constantly passes the cup.

A threesome of pros saw an old duffer waiting around. "Want to make a fourth?" they said.

"Sure," said he.

"We want to warn you. We're pros, and we play for a dollar a hole."

"That's all right, if you'll give me two lookouts," he said. Not knowing what that was, but thinking it innocent, they agreed. As the first man teed off, the old man screamed at the top of his voice, "Loookkkkout!" He never used the second one, of course, but won all 18 holes!

A pair of dub golfers were on the first tee. The first fairway was bordered by rows of trees. One of the dubs sliced so that the ball struck one of the trees, and without moving from his stance, he caught the ball on the rebound. Bewildered, he asked his friend, "What shall I do now?" Without hesitation a suggestion was made: "Tee it up, hit it again, and then put your hands in your pockets."

Two chubby duffers, ordered to play golf by their physicians, managed to get to the first tee. One duffer said, "I don't have the energy to play too long."

The other one said, "Okay. We'll quit as soon as either one of us gets a hole in one!"

Golf swings are like snowflakes. There are no two exactly alike.

Golf pro: Tee the ball.
Novice: Sure, I see it, but why the baby talk?

The rich duffer joined a foursome on the first tee. Two caddies stood behind him.

"Why did you bring two caddies?" one of his friends asked.

"Oh," the duffer said, "I always have to send one back to the clubhouse for laughing."

The duffer had been invited to play with three of the best players in the club. They were men who usually shot in the low 70s. The duffer was invited to tee off first. In his embarrassment at playing in such illustrious company, he completely missed his ball on his first swing. Trying even harder on his second swing, he missed in the same way. Feeling that he had to say something, he turned to the others and said: "Tough course, isn't it?"

The two golfers were introduced on the first tee. Before starting off one tried to arrange some sort of a match.

"My handicap is 14. What's yours?" he asked his new companion.

"A bad back, lumbago, weak wrists, and an incurable slice," came the ready response.

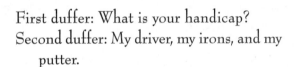

First duffer: What is your handicap?
Second duffer: My driver, my irons, and my putter.

First duffer: When you were playing golf, did you ever shoot a birdie?
Second duffer: No, but I once shot at a duck.

Two duffers were playing together. After the first hole, one said to the other, "What did you take on that hole?"

"I took a seven," the second duffer said. "What did you take?"

"I took a six," his friend said.

After they had finished the second hole, the first duffer said, "What did you—"

"Hey, not so fast," his friend said. "It's my turn to ask first."

Ladies' Day

Judy: What'd you buy George for his birthday?

Linda: This set of golf clubs.

Judy: That's a great idea. The bag is such a pretty pink. What are those cute booties for?

Linda: Oh, everybody knows that. They keep the woods covered.

Judy: Well, what're the numbers for?

Linda: Don't you know anything about golf? Those numbers tell you how many times to hit the ball.

Golfer's wife: Dear, I've swung at the ball 14 times and haven't hit it yet.

Golfer: Keep trying, dear. It's beginning to look a bit worried.

A man was playing golf with his wife who was in a talkative mood. He finally turned to her in disgust, "Please don't talk so much. You are driving me out of my mind."

"That's no drive," she said. "That's just a short putt."

Spring had come. At breakfast the golfer's wife said, "Now just because the weather is pretty today, don't think you're going to sneak off and play golf all day."

"Now, honey," he said, "don't get upset. Golf is the furthest thing from my mind. Would you please pass the toast and putter?"

Woman golfer, teeing off, to husband: "Now tell me if you notice anything I'm doing right."

A wife, to whom golf was a total mystery, never could understand why her husband insisted on tiring himself by walking so far every time he played.

One day, she went with him to see what the game was all about. She followed him until he landed in a bunker. There he floundered about for some time in the sand.

The lady seated herself on top of the bunker, took out her knitting, and said complacently, "There, I knew you could just as well play in one place if you made up your mind to!"

Two women joined each other on the golf links every month. On this particular day, one of the women strode to the first tee, pulled back her club, closed her eyes, and swung with all her might. The ball hooked off to the side, ricocheted off several trees, and took a fantastic bounce onto the green and into the cup for a hole in one. Her friend turned and frowned. "Sylvia, you sneak," she said angrily, "you've been practicing."

An avid golfer married a gal whose favorite hobby was attending auctions. Both talked in their sleep. From his side of the bed would come the mumbled warning: "Fore." And from her side the sleepy response: "Four twenty-five."

The club pro walked over to a duo of ladies and asked, "Do either of you want to learn how to play good golf?"

One of the women answered, "Maybe my friend would. I learned yesterday!"

When "fore" shouted twice didn't move the women on the green ahead, a fellow golfer suggested trying "3.98."

"Really, I can't play golf," said the dumb blonde. "I don't even know how to hold the caddie."

Two women were returning from their first attempt at bowling. The husband of one, an inveterate golfer, asked with a raised eyebrow: "How'd you make out?"

"Well," she said, "at least we didn't lose any balls."

Carlson's wife had never been on a golf course before. She waited patiently for her husband out on the clubhouse patio. Suddenly Carlson came running up to her and shouted jubilantly, "I just hit a hole in one."

"Did you?" asked his wife. "Do it again, dear, I didn't see you."

In a sporting goods store, a woman asked to see a "low handicap," explaining that her husband wanted one so much and she thought it would be nice to surprise him on his birthday.

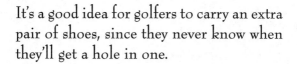

It's a good idea for golfers to carry an extra pair of shoes, since they never know when they'll get a hole in one.

Two women were chatting about their husbands. "My husband almost lost his mind over golf," the first woman said. "All he thought about was golf, golf, golf. He never played less than three days a week. His problem is so bad that he now visits a psychiatrist about it."

"Is the psychiatrist helping him?" her friend asked.

"I think he must be," the first woman said. "He and my husband play golf together every Tuesday, Thursday, and Saturday."

One woman explained why more women don't play golf. "We have more important things to lie about."

Plowing the Field

Q: Why is a golf course like Swiss cheese?
A: Because they both have holes in them.

First golfer: I played golf with Tiger Woods
the other day.
Second golfer: That's incredible. How did
it happen?
First golfer: Well, when I hit my ball off
the first tee, it went into the lake. The
guy standing beside me said, "Boy, if
you're a golfer, I'm Tiger Woods."

On the course last week, the foursome in front of us was so old they were settling up after every hole.

After an old duffer teed off, he asked me to comment on his form. I told him I've seen better swings in a condemned playground.

I understand more golf games have been won with pencils than were ever won with putters or drivers.

This golfer had been playing golf for years and he had the finest equipment, but his

technique never improved a bit. As his friend watched, he teed up at the first hole and promptly drove a brand-new ball into the woods. On the second hole, he drove another new ball into a lake. On the third, he lost a new ball in another part of the woods.

"Why don't you use an old ball?" his friend asked.

"I've never had an old ball," he said.

At a home-talent golf tournament the club secretary caught one of the members driving off about a foot in front of the teeing mark.

"Here!" he cried, indignantly. "You can't do that. You're disqualified!"

"What for?" demanded the golfer.

"Why, you just drove off in front of the mark."

The player looked at the secretary coldly. "Go back to the clubhouse," he said tersely. "I'm playing my third stroke."

First golfer: I'm anxious to make this shot.
    That's my mother-in-law up there on
    the clubhouse porch.
Second golfer: Don't be a fool. You can't
    hit her at 200 yards.

Expert: Knock the ball as near that flag as
    you can.
The ball landed within a foot of the hole.
Novice: What do I do next?
Expert: Knock it into the hole.
Novice: Into the hole? Why didn't you tell
    me that in the first place?

On a visit to Scotland, General Ulysses S. Grant was treated to a demonstration of a game he'd never heard of before, something called golf. His host wanted to show Grant how the game was played, even though he wasn't much of a golfer himself.

While Grant watched, the man placed a ball on a tee, stood back, and took a swing. Although he missed the ball, he did tear up a patch of grass. He tried again, with the same result. Again and again he sent patches of dirt and grass into the air without once hitting the ball.

Grant looked from his perspiring host to the ball, then back to his host. "There seems to be a fair amount of exercise in the game," he said. "But I fail to see the purpose of the ball."

You can always tell when the boss has retired. More members of the staff start to beat him.

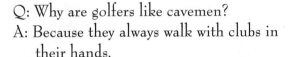

Q: Why are golfers like cavemen?
A: Because they always walk with clubs in
    their hands.

A golfer sliced his drive, and the ball went
through the windshield of a passing car.
The startled motorist lost control and hit
two other cars. Soon a policeman arrived,
surveyed the accident scene and found the
golfer standing by his ball on the road.

"What are you going to do about this?"
demanded the policeman.

"First thing," replied the golfer, "change
my grip."

Then there's the terrible temper type of golfer who says he can't afford to break 80...because golf clubs are too expensive these days.

When miracles happen on the golf course, it is important to know how to respond to them. At Pebble Beach, California, songwriter Hoagy Carmichael, who is an avid golfer, teed up on a par-three hole, picked up a club, and hit the ball. It bounced once on the green, went right to the pin, dropped in for a hole in one. Hoagy didn't say a word, but reached in his pocket, pulled out another ball, teed up, then observed, "I think I've got the idea now."

When I play golf I have a lot of style but I don't hit the ball far enough. What I'm trying to say is—I know how to address the ball; I just don't put enough stamps on it!

Golf is a game where when you don't suc-
ceed, you try, try again. And, if you're
honest, you mark it down on the scorecard.

A golfer returned home from a Saturday
round of golf and was greeted by his two
youngsters asking, "Daddy, did you win?"

"Well, children," he replied, "in golf it
doesn't matter so much if you win. But
your father got to hit the ball more times
than anyone else."

A golfer had been hit on the head by a long
drive and was lying in the center of the
fairway with a small crowd around him. As

he began to regain consciousness, one of the other players was trying to question him. "Are you married?" he asked the injured man.

"No," the fellow said, "this is the worst situation I've ever been in."

One day President Harding invited Grantland Rice and Ring Lardner to join him in a game of golf. Rice was a good player, but Lardner tended to hit the ball low and with a hook. Harding, on the other hand, had the habit of making his shot and then moving on ahead before the others had taken their turns. Thus it was that one of Lardner's shots just whistled past Harding's head and struck the branches of a tree over the President's head. Harding looked around in surprise and then with puzzlement that no apology from Lardner was forthcoming.

Instead, Lardner said, "Well, I did my best to make Coolidge the President of the United States."

Harding roared with laughter.

Golf is really a stupid game. I'm glad I don't have to play it again until next week.

Two Spanish detectives were standing over the body of Juan Gonzalez. "How was he shot?" inquired the first.

"I theenk eet was a golf gun," said the other.

"But what ees a golf gun?" asked his buddy.

"Who knows," came back the reply, "but eet sure made a hole in Juan."

There are two times to address a golf ball, before and after swinging.

More
Caddie Stories

Caddie: A golfing expert who loses balls for you in one round, so that he can find them for himself in the next.

Is it true that the first lie detector was a caddie?

A young broker, after a particularly brutal session in a sand trap, sought to relieve the uncomfortable silence by cheerily declaring to his caddie: "Funny game, golf."

The boy morosely replied: " 'Tain't meant to be."

Full of confidence, Mr. Blowhard looked down the fairway and casually told his caddie: "This should be good for a long drive and a putt." With that, he took a mighty swing, hit the sod, and the ball rolled only a few feet.

"Boy," said the caddie, "this is going to be one heck of a putt."

Irate golfer: You must be the world's worst caddie!

Caddie: Hardly. That would be too much of a coincidence.

Red: Donald's got a job as a caddie for a
    golf club. Is there much money in that?
Fred: The salary ain't much, but they make
    a lot extra backin' up fellas when they
    lie about their scores.

Golfer: I'd move heaven and earth to break
    100.
Caddie: Try heaven, you've already moved
    enough earth today.

As Richardson came out on the eighteenth
for a score well over 100, he turned to his
caddie and said, "I'll never be able to hold
my head up again."

  "Oh, I don't know, sir," came the reply.
"You've been doing it all afternoon."

Many golfers use carts instead of caddies because carts can't count, criticize, or laugh.

Golfer: What can I do to prevent me from topping all my drives?
Caddie: Turn the ball upside down.

Golfer *(far off in the rough)*: Say, caddie, why do you keep looking at your watch?
Caddie: It isn't a watch, sir; it's a compass.

Golfer: Well, caddie, how do you like my game?

Caddie: I suppose it's all right, but I still prefer golf.

Golfer: Boy, how many did I take to do that hole?

Caddie: I'm sorry, sir, I only went to a primary school.

Golfer: This is the toughest course I ever played on.

Caddie: Sir, how can you tell? You haven't even been on the course yet.

The golfer, annoyed at the loss of his ball, started to scold his caddie for not having been more careful in watching its flight.

Attempting to excuse himself, the caddie said, "Well, sir, it don't usually go anywhere, so it sort of took me unprepared like."

Real devotees of the game of golf are fanatics of a peculiar breed. There was the case of such a man, who returned home after a long day on the links. His wife greeted him, and observed that their young son, Filbert, had come in only a moment before. "He says he's been caddying for you all day."

"Is that so?" replied the sportsman. "Somehow I thought that boy seemed mighty familiar."

An irate golfer threw away his last club. The caddie watched, then said, "How about your sweater? Will you be wanting that?"

The caddie was suffering from a severe case of hiccups. He was making a nervous wreck of the golfer he was caddying for. On the eighth hole, the golfer missed a birdie putt by three inches. He couldn't control himself any longer. He turned to the caddie and shouted, "You and your hiccups! See what you caused me to do?"

"But I didn't hiccup when you were putting," said the caddie.

"I know it," cried the golfer, "but I allowed for it."

Golf
Is Religious

A minister went out to play one afternoon. On the fifth hole he missed a putt by a tenth of an inch. He shook his head and said, "Drat."

His caddie said, "Padre, cursing like that, you'll never break par!"

A certain preacher was chagrined by the fact that one of his friends and golfing companions invariably beat him. His companion, an older man, said, "Don't take it too hard. You win in the end. You'll probably be burying me one of these days."

"I know," said the preacher, "but even then it will be your hole."

An assistant pastor was watching while a member of the congregation was beating the minister at golf. He walked over to the fellow and whispered in his ear, "Remember the cloth, sir."

"Cloth?" answered the congregant. "This is golf, not billiards."

A lot of ministers don't play golf because they don't have the vocabulary for it.

I was standing near the eighteenth green of our golf course when a foursome came off, and one of the men apologized to a clergyman, who was part of the group, for his

occasional bad language. "But sir," he added, "how do you let off steam when you miss a shot or get frustrated?"

The response was simple. "I just repeat the names of some of the members of my congregation—with feeling!"

A distinguished clergyman and one of his parishioners were playing golf. It was a very close match, and at the last hole the clergyman teed up, addressed the ball, and swung his driver with great force. The ball, instead of sailing down the fairway, merely rolled off the tee and settled slowly some twelve feet away.

The clergyman frowned, glared, and bit his lip, but said nothing. His opponent regarded him for a moment, and then remarked: "Doctor, that is the most profane silence I have ever witnessed."

The marble tournament was in full swing. One little boy had missed an easy shot, and let slip a real cuss word.

"Henry!" called the preacher from the spectator's bench, "what do little boys who swear when they are playing marbles turn into?"

"Golfers," little Henry replied.

A preacher one day decided to take up golfing. On his first swing at the ball, it sailed into a clump of trees. A moment later, a big bird flew out of the trees, circled the ground, and dropped the ball neatly into the cup.

Looking up the preacher cried, "But Father, please, I'd rather do it myself."

The pastor was out on the course with one of his flock. The man was given to quick bursts of temper and well-chosen cusswords when the ball didn't bounce well for him. Unable to stand the profanity, the pastor said, "I've played golf with some of the finest players in the country. Last week I played with a man who went six under par for this course. I didn't hear one word of profanity from him."

The player said, "What did he have to curse about?"

For several years, a minister and a professor had regularly played golf together. They were evenly matched and there was a keen rivalry. Then one spring the professor's game suddenly improved so much that the minister was regularly beaten. The preacher's efforts to improve his own game were unsuccessful, but finally he came up with an idea. He went to the bookstore, picked out three how-to-play-golf texts,

and had them sent to the professor for a birthday present. It wasn't long before they were evenly matched again.

A pastor was playing golf with some men from his church. After hitting his ball in the sand trap for the third time, he turned, red-faced and exasperated, and said, "Won't one of you laymen please say a few appropriate words?"

Life Is Like a Round of Golf

Life is like a round of golf
With many a turn and twist.
But the game is much too sweet and short
To curse the shots you've missed.

Sometimes you'll hit it straight and far,
Sometimes the putts roll true.
But each round has its errant shots
And troubles to play through.

So always swing with courage
No matter what the lie.
And never let the hazards
Destroy the joy inside.

And keep a song within your heart.
Give thanks that you can play.
For the round is much too short and sweet
To let it slip away.

—CRISWELL FREEMAN

Fairway Fun

Bob couldn't find his golf ball. Finally, out of desperation, he sneaked a new ball out of his pocket and dropped it on the ground when his partner wasn't looking. "Dave, I've found it!"

"You cheater!" said Dave. "How dare you! I never thought you'd stoop to cheating for a mere dollar!"

"What do you mean 'cheater'?" Bob said indignantly. "I found my ball, I'll play it where it lies!"

"I can prove that's not your ball," said Dave triumphantly, "because I've been standing on your ball for five minutes!"

A man came home from playing golf and announced to his wife, "I'm never playing golf with Bill again."

"Why not?" she asked. "He's been your friend for years."

"Would you continue to play with a guy who always loses so many balls that other groups are always playing through, tells lousy jokes while you are trying to putt, and generally offends everyone around him on the course?"

"I should say not."

"Well, neither would he."

Three senior golfers were griping continually.

"The fairways are too long," said one.

"The hills are too high," said another.

"The bunkers are too deep," complained the third.

Finally an 80-year-old put things into perspective. "At least," he noted, "we're on the right side of the grass."

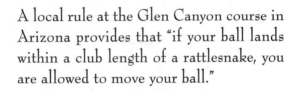

A local rule at the Glen Canyon course in Arizona provides that "if your ball lands within a club length of a rattlesnake, you are allowed to move your ball."

On this particular Saturday morning, Terry was playing a round of golf by himself when all of a sudden the ghost of his old business partner appeared before him. "Gary, is that you?" the astonished Terry asked.

"Yes, Terry, it's me, your old partner. I've been in heaven since I died two years ago."

"Gosh, Gary. What's it like up there?"

"Well, there are some good things and some bad things about heaven. The golf courses are magnificent. Rolling fairways, lush greens, beautiful clubhouses, and you never have to wait."

Terry scratched his head. "All that sounds great. What could possibly be bad about it?"

The ghost looked at Terry. "You and I have a tee time of 8:00 tomorrow."

Hawkins, at 87, was the oldest club member, but despite a hip replacement, near deafness, arthritis, and various other ailments, he still managed a round of golf each day. On one recent morning Hawkins putted on the ninth green, and as his caddie picked up his ball the boy said, "I'll put you down for a ten on that hole, Mr. Hawkins."

"What's that, son? Speak up, please," said Hawkins. "And make that a seven!"

While breaking in a new caddie, Julius Boros told him to pick up a big divot he had just made. Continuing down the course, Boros reminded the boy to pick up every

divot. Around the fourteenth hole, the caddie was gasping and dragging the bag.

"What's wrong?" Boros asked.

"Mr. Boros, what do you want me to do with all these divots?"

A salesman was leaving the office for a round of golf when his boss stopped him.

"Williams, if you spend all your time on the golf course, you won't have anything put aside for a rainy day."

"Of course I will, boss. My desk is piled up with work I've put aside for a rainy day!"

Mrs. Moore and her caddie were searching for her ball when the caddie pointed to a ball in the rough. "There's your ball, Mrs. Moore," he said.

"That can't be my ball," protested Mrs. Moore. "It looks far too old."

"But, ma'am," the caddie retorted, "it's been a long, long time since we started."

"So, son, what are you going to do with your life now that you've graduated from college?" asked Norman.

"I've given it some thought, Dad," replied the young man. "And I've decided to just play golf every day."

"Are you crazy?" said Norman. "Do you think I'd allow any son of mine to spend his life running around a golf course?"

"Of course not, Dad. I was hoping you'd buy me a golf cart."

Links Laughter

Chi Chi Rodriguez, relating his caddie's advice on a putt: "He told me to keep the ball low."

The two women were put together as partners in the club tournament and met on the putting green for the first time.

After introductions, the first golfer asked, "What's your handicap?"

"Oh, I'm a scratch golfer," the other replied.

"Really!" exclaimed the first woman, suitably impressed that she was paired up with her.

"Yes, I write down all my good scores and scratch out all the bad ones!"

Cornford was searching through the woods for his lost ball when he stumbled upon another golfer from the adjoining fairway apparently doing the same thing. After the two of them had been poking around in the underbrush for a minute or so, the golfer yelled out, "Are you looking for a Wilson?"

"No, I'm looking for a Carlton," Cornford yelled back.

"Carlton? Is that your ball?"

"Who said anything about a ball?" bellowed Cornford. "Carlton is my caddie."

First golfer: I have the greatest golf ball in the world. You can't lose it.

Second golfer: How so?

First golfer: If you hit it into the sand, it beeps. If you hit it into the water, it floats. If you want to play golf at night, it glows.

Second golfer: Hey, sounds good. Where
    did you get it?
First golfer: Found it in the woods.

When President Dwight Eisenhower would
putt on the White House lawn, squirrels
would interfere with his practice. Ike had
them trapped and removed.

Richard and Ted were two of the bitterest
golf rivals in the retirement community.
Neither man trusted the other's arithmetic.
One day they were playing a heated match
and watching each other like hawks.

After holing out on the fourth green and
marking his six on the scorecard, Richard
asked his opponent, "What'd you have?"

Ted went through the motions of men-
tally counting up. "Six!" he said and then
hastily corrected himself. "No—a five."

Calmly Richard marked the scorecard, saying out loud, "Eight!"

"Eight? I couldn't have had eight."

"Nope. You claimed six, then changed it to five. But actually you had seven."

"Then why mark down an eight?"

"One stroke penalty," said Richard, "for improving your lie."

Willard and Clarence were annoyed by an unusually elderly twosome in front of them. One of the pair diddled and dawdled on the fairway, while the other was searching diligently through the rough.

"Hey," shouted Willard impatiently, "why don't you help your friend find his ball?"

"He's got his ball," replied the old man. "He's looking for his club."

"You know that partner I got paired with today?" asked Art. "He was so bad he even lost his ball in the washer."

First golfer: So, is that new member any
    good at golf?
Second golfer: Absolutely. He's so good he
    doesn't have to cheat!

I'm on a golf kick. When he mentions golf, I kick him.

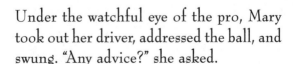

Under the watchful eye of the pro, Mary took out her driver, addressed the ball, and swung. "Any advice?" she asked.

"Well, I think your ball will go farther if you take the hood cover off the driver."

Sally returned home with a big smile on her face. Her husband, hard at work in the garden, looked up as she got out of her car. "You're smiling, Sally. You must have had a great round of golf."

Sally shook her head. "No. But for the first time I found more balls than I lost."

Thoughts from the Back Nine

Golf is a game in which you claim the privileges of age and retain the playthings of youth.

—SAMUEL JOHNSON

Gerry Ford was the first person to make golf a contact sport. When he yelled, "Fore!" you never knew if he was telling people to get out of the way or predicting how many spectators he was going to hit.

—BOB HOPE

My wife always said she wanted to marry a millionaire. Well, she made me a millionaire. I used to be a multimillionaire.

—CHI CHI RODRIGUEZ

I'm not saying my golf game went bad, but if I grew tomatoes, they'd come up sliced.

—LEE TREVINO

I owe everything to golf. Where else could a guy with an IQ like mine make this much money?

—HUBERT GREEN

I was three over: one over a house, one over a patio, and one over a swimming pool.

—GEORGE BRETT

I'm about five inches from being an out-standing golfer. That's the distance my left ear is from my right.

—BEN CRENSHAW

Pressure is playing for ten dollars when you don't have a dime in your pocket.

—LEE TREVINO

A peculiarity of golf is that what you aim
at you generally miss.

—Rex Lardner

The money is completely unimportant—
once you have won enough of it.

—Johnny Miller

The difference between golf and government
is that in golf you can't improve your lie.

—George Deukmejian

I never wanted to be a millionaire. I just
wanted to live like one.

—Walter Hagen

Golfers have analyzed the game in order to find "the secret." There is no secret.

—HENRY COTTON

I've had a good day when I don't fall out of the cart.

—BUDDY HACKETT

The only time my prayers are never answered is on the golf course.

—BILLY GRAHAM

It's okay to have butterflies. Just get them
flying in formation.

—FRANCISCO LOPEZ

The most exquisitely satisfying act in the
world of golf is that of throwing a club.

—HENRY LONGHURST

In golf, I'm one under. One under a tree,
one under a rock, one under a bush....

—GERRY CHEEVERS

It took me 17 years to get 3,000 hits in baseball. I did it in one afternoon on the golf course.   —HANK AARON

How has retirement affected my golf game? A lot more people beat me now.

—DWIGHT EISENHOWER

I'll know I'm getting better at golf because I'm hitting fewer spectators.

—GERALD FORD

Golf is a game where you yell "fore," shoot six, and write down five.

—PAUL HARVEY

The difference between a sand trap and water is the difference between a car crash and an airplane crash. You have a chance of recovering from a car crash.

—BOBBY JONES

Never gamble with a stranger, and if you do and he stops arguing the handicap too soon, you know you have a hawk in the chicken yard.

—SAM SNEAD

Golf is not a funeral, though both can be very sad affairs.

—BERNARD DARWIN

Bad putting stems from thinking how instead of where.

—Jackie Burke Jr.

One minute you have total volition and willpower. Next minute, you can't tie your own shoelaces.

—Mac O'Grady

Whenever I play with Gerald Ford, I try to make it a foursome—the President, myself, a paramedic, and a faith healer.

—Bob Hope

Golf is a funny game. One day you think you're the best in the world and the next you feel like nothing.

—CHI CHI RODRIGUEZ

Innumerable times I've had golfers come to me complaining about some fault that is ruining their swings….A goodly number of these victims will begin telling me what's wrong with their swings. They don't seem to realize that if they knew what was wrong, they wouldn't be coming to me and paying me for an expert diagnosis and cure.

—TOMMY ARMOUR

They say golf is like life but don't believe them. Golf is more complicated than that.

—GARDNER DICKINSON

Practice is the only golf advice that is good for everybody.

—ARNOLD PALMER

Ninety percent of putts that are short don't go in.

—YOGI BERRA

Other Books by Bob Phillips

42 Days to Feeling Great!

The All-New Clean Joke Book

*Awesome Animal Jokes
for Kids*

*The Awesome Book
of Bible Trivia*

*Awesome Good Clean Jokes
for Kids*

*The Best of the
Good Clean Jokes*

*Bob Phillips' Encyclopedia
of Good Clean Jokes*

*A Classic Collection of Golf
Jokes and Quotes*

*Controlling Your Emotions
Before They Control You*

*Extremely Good Clean
Jokes for Kids*

Good Clean Jokes for Kids

*Goofy Good Clean
Jokes for Kids*

How Can I Be Sure?

In Search of Bible Trivia

*Jest Another Good Clean
Joke Book*

Over the Hill & on a Roll

*Phillips' Awesome Collection of
Quips and Quotes*

Redi-Reference

*Super-Duper Good Clean Jokes
for Kids*

*Totally Cool Clean Jokes
for Kids*

*Ultimate Good Clean Jokes
for Kids*

*The World's Greatest Collection
of Clean Jokes*

*The World's Greatest Collection
of Knock-Knock Jokes for Kids*

For information on how to purchase any of the above books, contact
your local bookstore or send a self-addressed stamped envelope to:
Family Services
P.O. Box 9363
Fresno, CA 93702

The only time a golfer tells the truth is when he calls another golfer a liar.

First golfer: Charlie plays a fair game of
    golf, doesn't he?
Second golfer: Yes, if you watch him.

Golfer: Why is golf like fishing?
Golf pro: They both mysteriously encourage
    exaggeration.

The caddie laughed at the golfer's vain attempt to contact the ball.

"If you laugh at me again," the man shouted, "I'll hit you over the head with this club."

The caddie admitted, "Maybe you could at that—it is a little larger than the ball."

Last week I played with my boss. On the first tee, he topped the ball and it landed 50 feet away from the tee and 300 from the green. I conceded the putt.

"It's not that I cheat," the golfer explained, "but the lower my scores are, the better I feel—and I'm playing for my health, you know."

One golfer to another: First it was my marriage. Now the magic has gone out of my nine iron.

Golfer: Who invented golf and said it was fun?
Golf pro: The same guy who invented bagpipes and said it was music.

Golf is an outdoor game played with the head and hands; the head is on the club and the hands are on the golfer.

Golf is a sport where some people say, "Two can live as cheaply as one can play golf."

A golf ball is a small object which remains on the tee while a perspiring citizen fans it vigorously with a long club.

Golfer to golfer: "Speaking of the credibility gap—what's your handicap?"

I'm not exactly a great golfer. I have no particular handicap—I'm all handicap.

I called up a friend and asked him to play. He said, "Sorry—we already have a three-some."

One of the best ways to help a man get out of the woods is to find the golf ball he's looking for.

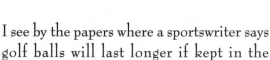

I see by the papers where a sportswriter says golf balls will last longer if kept in the refrigerator. Sure they will! Taking them out on the course and smacking them around is what wears them out.

Explorer: Savages surrounded us. They uttered awful cries and beat their clubs upon the ground.

Weary listener: Golfers, probably.

Q: What did the dentist say to the golfer?
A: You have a hole in one.

This morning I missed a hole in one by eight strokes!

First golfer: My wife doesn't mind my playing golf every Wednesday afternoon just as long as I get home by six-thirty.

Second golfer: I have to be home by six. My wife's a half hour meaner than yours.

Sign at a golf club in Scotland:
Do not pick up lost balls until they have stopped rolling.

A man was on the verge of a nervous breakdown. His psychiatrist advised him to take up golf to get his mind off his business. Six months later the doctor advised him to take up business in order to get his mind off golf.

Ever notice that there seems to be a limit to almost everything except the number of wrong ways a golf ball can be hit?

A hysterical golfer raced into the club-house and said he had just killed his wife. "I didn't know she was behind me and the club hit her right in the head."

"What were you swinging?"

"A number three wood."

"Yeah. That one always gives me trouble too."

Last year the Russians invented a game that resembles golf. I think I've been playing it for years!

The real test in golf and in life is not in keeping out of the rough, but in getting out after we are in.

Two ants lived in an anthill on the first tee of a famous golf course. One day an inept golfer took a swing, missed the ball, and lifted a huge chunk of sod far into the air. As the ants watched, he swung again and sent a divot flying, which almost struck the ants.

As the duffer prepared to take his third swing, one ant turned to his companion and said, "If we want to get out of this alive, we'd better get on the ball."

First golfer: I think golf is a rich man's game.
Second golfer: Nonsense. Look at all the poor players!

Sunday Golf

Wife: Golf! Golf! Golf! I believe I'd drop
    dead if you spent one Sunday at home!
Golfer: Now, now, you know you can't bribe
    me.

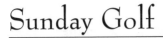

A minister glared at one of his parishioners and said, "I understand you went to
a golf game Sunday instead of to church."

    "That's a lie, Reverend, and I've got a fish
to prove it."

Sunday is the day when most of us bow our
heads. Some of us are praying and some
of us are playing golf.

If you want to be good at golf, you have to be serious about it. Some men play golf religiously—every Sunday.

Jones had just flubbed his fourth shot in the same trap one Sunday morning. "The way I'm playing golf," he muttered disgustedly, "I might just as well have gone to church."

You can always tell the golfers in church. When they put their hands together to pray, they use an interlocking grip.

A really good golfer is one who goes to church on Sunday…first.

Member: Reverend, is it a sin to play golf on Sunday?
Reverend: In your case, it's a sin every day.

I always have great difficulty deciding whether to play golf or go to church on Sunday. For example, last Sunday I had to flip a coin 27 times.

Soft Pencil,
Soft Conscience

First golfer: Those are my brand-new
$1.25 golf balls you're losing.
Second golfer: Look here, if you can't
afford this game, you shouldn't be
playing it.

Golf pro: Now just go through the motions
without driving the ball.
Golfer: That's precisely what I'm trying to
overcome.

Every golfer is a combination of good attributes and bad. When you play golf, you should be kind and gracious to your opponent and think only of his sterling qualities. You should try to overlook any slight flaw in his character. Remember that he, too, is a human being with the same frustrations and disappointments and problems that you have. You should not make harsh judgments just because he happens to be a dirty low-down rascal who is three up on you.

First golfer: My doctor tells me I can't play golf.
Second golfer: So he's played with you too.

First golfer: Do you play golf?
Second golfer: No, but I can't give it up.

Slow, elderly golfer: Let me tell you, young
   fella, that I was playing this game
   before you were born.
Impatient opponent: Well, would you mind
   trying to finish before I die?

First older golfer: I'm losing my eyesight.
   Would you mind watching my ball?
Second older golfer: Not at all. Matter of
   fact, I have excellent eyesight.
First older golfer: Did you see where it
   went?
Second older golfer: Sure did! I saw exactly
   where it went.
First older golfer: Where'd it go?
Second older golfer: I can't remember.

While playing a short hole, a golfer hit his drive into the rough, where it flushed up a bird. It was, he admitted, the first time he'd seen a partridge in a par three.

First golfer: Why do you wear two pairs of pants when you play golf?
Second golfer: In case I get a hole in one!

There was once a Scot who had played golf with the same ball for 30 years. One day he lost it and was forced to buy another. He walked into the local sports shop and said, "Well, here I am again."

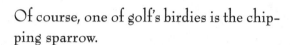

Of course, one of golf's birdies is the chipping sparrow.

First golfer's wife: My husband is very frank and plainspoken. He always calls a spade a spade.

Second golfer's wife: So does mine. But I can't tell you what he sometimes calls his golf clubs.

By the time a man can afford to lose a ball, he can't hit it that far.

A highly competitive foursome was going around the golf course on a sweltering summer day. One of the group had a sun-stroke—and the others made him count it.

My golf is improving. Now I miss the ball much closer than I used to.

Well, people make fun of us golf enthusi-asts. But the way I figure it, there must be time for both work and play. And if you watch a game, it's fun. If you play it, it's recreation. If you work at it, it's golf.

A golf ball is a golf ball—no matter how you putt it.

First golfer: How do you do? Would you like to play a round with me?

Second golfer: Why, yes, I would.

First golfer: What do you play the course in?

Second golfer: I play a 69.

First golfer: Well, I was going to place some bets but let's forget that.

They played for seven holes and the first golfer was floored at how poorly the second golfer was playing. He was taking stroke after stroke.

Second golfer: Well, that's it. I'll see you later.

First golfer: What do you mean, you will see me later? We're only on the seventh hole. Why are you quitting?

Second golfer: I told you when we started that I play a 69 game. I have had my 69 strokes and I'm going in. Someday I may finish the course.

I played Civil War golf. I went out in 61 and came back in 65.

Two business partners were playing a round of golf one day. On the third tee, one said to the other, "Wait, I think I forgot to take the cash box."

His friend responded, "So what? We're both here, aren't we?"

I'm an ordinary sort of fellow—42 around the chest, 42 around the waist, 96 around the golf course.

—GROUCHO MARX

First golfer: Funny golf socks you're
    wearing—one yellow and the other green.
Second golfer: What's so funny? Got
    another pair just like 'em at home.

"It's a dirty lie!" said the golfer as he came
upon his ball which had fallen right into
the middle of a mud hole.

Nurse: Who are they operating on today?
Orderly: A fellow who had a golf ball
    knocked down his throat at the links.
Nurse: And who is the man waiting so ner-
    vously in the hall? A relative?
Orderly: No, that's the golfer. He's waiting
    for his ball.

Man to friend: "After three sets of clubs and ten years of lessons, I'm finally getting some fun out of golf. I quit."

First golfer: I hear you play golf. What do
   you go round in?
Second golfer: Well, usually I wear a
   sweater.

Golfer: A man who hits and tells.

Golfer: A man who roughly speaking, plays golf roughly speaking.

Golfer: A man who must have endurance—and so must their listeners.

Golfer: A man who has one advantage over the fisherman. He doesn't have to show anything to prove it.

All golfers are entitled to life, liberty, and the pursuit of golf balls.

Many a man whose doctor advised him to play golf has an instructor who advises him to quit.

Extreme Golf

A golfer rushed up to the foursome ahead of him and said, "Do you mind if I play through? I just had an urgent message. My wife was injured in an automobile accident and has been rushed to the hospital."

First golfer: Shall we play again next Saturday?
Second golfer: Well, I was going to get married on Saturday, but I can put it off.

As an avid golfer, I prefer to have the course to myself on weekends and think

nothing of teeing off with my foursome at 5 A.M. One Saturday I met my match. As we played, a twosome bore down on us from behind. Catching up on the sixth tee, one of them came over to ask if they could play through.

"I'm getting married at nine o'clock this morning," he explained, "and I'd like to get in 18 holes before the wedding."

—HARRY G. NICOLL

Man in golf cart to players ahead: "May I play through? My batteries are low."

Then there's the story of the thoughtful wife. She died early in the week so her funeral wouldn't interfere with her husband's Saturday golf game.

The young man had just teed up on the first hole, and was getting ready to drive when a woman in a wedding dress came running toward him. She grabbed his arm and began shouting as she pulled him toward the parking lot.

"For heaven's sake," the man screamed back, "I said only if it rains!"

A man was showing his friend a new set of matched golf clubs he had just bought. "Doctor's orders," the man told his friend. "My wife and I have been gaining too much weight and we went to see the doctor about it. He said we needed more exercise, so I joined the country club and bought myself this set of golf clubs."

"What about your wife?" the friend asked. "What did you buy her?"

"A new lawn mower," the golfer said.

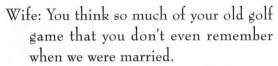

Wife: You think so much of your old golf
 game that you don't even remember
 when we were married.
Husband: Of course, I do, my dear; it was
 the day I sank that 30-foot putt.

A foursome of golfers always managed to
be in by 6 P.M. One day they were a full
hour late. When they came in, the pro
inquired, "Whatever happened that you fellows were so late today?"

 "Well," replied one, "everything was okay
until the fourth tee, and then Frank had a
stroke and died. After that it was hit the
ball, drag Frank, hit the ball, drag Frank."

Wife to husband at front door carrying golf clubs: "You don't have to go all the way to the golf course for a hole in one. There's one in the roof, one in the screen door, and one in the...."

A Nice Walk in the Woods

"It's true," the weekend golfer told his wife on his way out the door, "I love golf more than I love you. But," he proclaimed, "I love you more than tennis."

The way I see it, golf is just an expensive way to play marbles.

First golfer: Did the tournament committee approve your scorecard?
Second golfer: No. I just asked for the fictional rights.

Club manager: I'm sorry, sir, but we don't have any open time on the course today.

Golfer: Yeah? What if Jack Nicklaus and Tiger Woods showed up? I'll bet you would find a tee time for them.

Club manager: Of course we would.

Golfer: Well, I just happen to know they are not coming, so I'll take their time.

Golf is a game that requires the nerves of a man who can look an opponent straight in the eye and say calmly, "That was a practice swing."

A stomach specialist from a big city has a formula for patients with nervous indigestion. He asks them if they play golf. If they say yes, he tells them to cut it out. If they say no, he tells them to start playing.

When some senior golfers talk about their scores, you don't know the half of it.

A golfer was talking to his friend: "You know how late it was when we left the clubhouse yesterday? Well, when I got home my wife didn't say a word about me being late. She had dinner waiting for me and after that she wouldn't even let me help with the dishes. She made me sit in the living room and she brought my pipe and slippers and told me to be comfortable while I read the evening paper."

"How much damage had she done to the car?"

A golfer was playing with friends at a course where he had never played before. His first swing missed the ball completely. His second swing, even harder than the first, missed exactly like the previous one. He was terribly embarrassed and felt he had to make some sort of excuse. He looked at his friends and said, "Boy, what do you think about that? This course is two inches lower than the one I usually play on."

There's nothing like a game of golf to quiet your nerves, build your muscles, increase your stamina, and strengthen your resolve... just in case you ever decide to play again.

The expectant mother who was being rushed to the hospital didn't quite make it. Instead she gave birth to her baby on the hospital lawn. Later the father received a

bill listing the delivery room fee as $65. Disturbed about it, he complained to the hospital bookkeeping department. He reminded them that his wife gave birth to the baby on the front lawn.

By return mail he received a corrected bill which read, "Greens fee, $65."

First golfer: I can't see why you play golf with him. He's a bad loser.
Second golfer: I'd rather play with a bad loser than a winner any time.

An army general was playing golf like a true military man. Every time he got on the green, he stroked the ball toward the hole and yelled—"Fall in!"

My doctor told me to play 36 holes a day, so I went out and bought a harmonica.

I shoot golf in the low 70s—until I get to the fifth hole.

First golfer: How's your daughter's golf?
Second golfer: Oh, she's going around in less and less every day.
First golfer: Yes, I know, but how's her golf?

Sammy Davis, Jr. was asked about his handicap when he played golf with Bob Hope. He said, "I'm black, I'm Jewish, and I have one eye—any other questions?"

Sign on fence bordering golf course: "Attention, golfers. We are raising small children behind this fence, so please refrain from enriching their vocabularies. Thank you!"

A very formal minister went out to learn to play golf. He was very earnest but a poor golfer. Deciding that his game might be improved, he hired an instructor to teach him the finer points.

One day, while practicing on a golf course, he missed when teeing off. He tried three or four times, but each time his club hit several inches behind the ball. His instructor watched silently. Finally, the minister, becoming disgusted, glared at the stationary ball. He muttered, "Tut, tut!"

Gravely the instructor walked toward him. "Sir," he said, "you'll never learn to play golf with those words."

A new member of a golf club was led to the first tee. Surrounded by grinning spectators, he teed off, and with an almost miraculous drive, landed the ball in the first hole. Noticing no sign of anything from his watchers, who were in fact struck speechless by this feat, he marched off to the second tee. Taking his stance he again drove at the ball, and again it went into the cup.

Waving his club as though in near disappointment he said, "Gosh, I sure thought I'd missed it that time."

Ralph Nader had some golf clubs recalled. They weren't up to par.

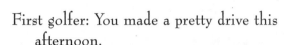

First golfer: You made a pretty drive this afternoon.
Second golfer: Which one do you mean?
First golfer: The one where you hit the ball.

I'm a two-handicap golfer—I have a boss who won't let me off early and a wife who keeps me home on weekends.

Last Sunday while I was playing golf a man hit me with a golf ball. I said, "That will cost you five dollars."

The man said, "Well, I yelled 'Fore'!"
And I said, "I'll take four instead."

Do you know some fellows play golf on weekends to forget their business troubles while others work all week trying to forget their lousy weekend golf scores?

Ben Hogan, all-time golfing great, was foiled by fate one day when he tried to give a duffer the thrill of a lifetime. Ben and a friend were playing a practice round. They had just holed out on a short three-par hole whose green was partially surrounded by trees and traps, when suddenly, out of nowhere, a ball plopped down and trickled within two inches of the cup.

As Hogan playfully tapped the ball in, a red-faced player came puffing from the direction of the deepest trap. Hogan held out his hand and said, "Mister, you're in for

the biggest kick you ever got out of golf. Just look in that cup."

The player followed directions and then hollered to a partner still hidden from view, "Hey, Joe, whaddya know! I sank it for a seven!"

A fair golfer is one who putts after 18 holes or 90 strokes—whichever comes first. I'm thinking of giving up golf—I can't break 90 even when I cheat.

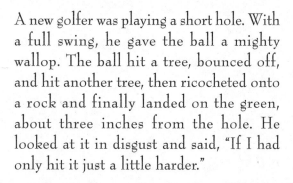

A new golfer was playing a short hole. With a full swing, he gave the ball a mighty wallop. The ball hit a tree, bounced off, and hit another tree, then ricocheted onto a rock and finally landed on the green, about three inches from the hole. He looked at it in disgust and said, "If I had only hit it just a little harder."

Two golfers looked up in time to see an atomic bomb demolish the distant city.

"Go ahead and putt," said one. "It'll be a few minutes before the shock wave hits us."

Two men were beginning a game of golf. The first man stepped to the tee and his first drive gave him a hole in one. The second man stepped up to the tee and said, "Okay, now I'll take my practice swing and then we'll start the game."

First golfer: My wife told me a month ago that if I didn't give up golf, she was going to pack up and leave me.

Second golfer: My, that's terrible.
First golfer: Yes, it is. It sure is lonesome
   around the house at night.

First golfer: Isn't Joe out of the bunker yet?
   How many strokes has he had?
Second golfer: Fifteen club and one
   apoplectic!

Two men reached the ninth hole of a dif-
ficult course. The hazard on the hole was
a ravine about as deep as the Grand
Canyon. One player managed to get his
ball on the green. The other watched his
ball disappear into the darkness of the
ravine. Rather than take the penalty, the
player went down to play out his ball. As
the sun sank in the west, the ball finally
bobbed out onto the green. A moment

later, the player appeared and said, "Not bad for three strokes."

His partner said, "I heard at least six strokes."

The player said, "Three of them were echoes."

Golfer's Psalm

My golf clubs are my inequity;
I shall want them no more;
My driver maketh my ball to slice into
green pastures;
My wedge causeth it to sink in still waters;
my mid-iron tempteth me, and I creep the
fairway to the sand trap for my ball's sake.
Yea, though I cross the creek in nine, I
dubbeth my approach. My putt runneth
over.
My ball is ever near me, its presence con-
foundeth me.
My clubs and my balls maketh me to pre-
pare a feast for mine enemies, verily. I am
their meal ticket.
Surely, I shall swing my clubs, cursing
them, all the days of my life, and I shall
shooteth a hundred forever.

Slices of Wisdom

It's not just enough to swing at the ball.
You've got to loosen your girdle and really
let the ball have it.

—BABE DIDRIKSON ZAHARIAS

Time goes by and people forget all the
tournaments I've won. Only my wife and
my dog remember.

—GARY PLAYER

Golf is like a love affair: if you don't take
it seriously, it's not fun; if you do take it
seriously, it breaks your heart.

—ARNOLD DALY

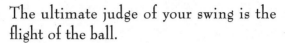

The ultimate judge of your swing is the
flight of the ball.

—BEN HOGAN

The reason the pro tells you to keep your
head down is so you can't see him laughing.

—PHYLLIS DILLER

Golf is mostly a game of failures.

—TOMMY ARMOUR

Golf is assuredly a mystifying game. It would seem that if a person has hit a golf ball correctly a thousand times, he should be able to duplicate the performance at will. But this is certainly not the case.

—BOBBY JONES

Life may not be fair, but golf is downright malicious.

—JIM MURRAY

If you are going to throw a club, it is important to throw it ahead of you—down the fairway, so you don't have to waste energy going back to pick it up.

—TOMMY BOLT

Golf is a good walk spoiled.

—MARK TWAIN

One time at Chattanooga I hit a real pretty iron to the green, and danged if my ball didn't hit a bobwhite in the air and knock it dead. My ball stopped about a foot from the cup and I knocked it in. Only time I ever made two birdies on the same hole.

—SAM SNEAD

Start each hole with an awareness that there may be subtle or mysterious elements waiting to sabotage your game.

—ROBERT TRENT JONES JR.

Golf is 20 percent mechanics and technique. The other 80 percent is philosophy, humor, tragedy, romance, melodrama, companionship, camaraderie, cussedness, and conversation.

—GRANTLAND RICE

Don't play too much golf. Two rounds a day are plenty.

—HARRY VARDON

Golf isn't a game, it's a curse. It wasn't created by the shepherds of St. Andrews but by the witches from *Macbeth*.

—ART SPANDER

I'm a golfaholic. And all the counseling in the world wouldn't help me.

—LEE TREVINO

I'm hitting the woods great, but I'm having trouble getting out of them.

—HARRY TOSCANO

The ardent golfer would play Mount Everest if somebody would put a flagstick on top.

—PETE DYE

Thinking must be the hardest thing to do in golf, because we do so little of it.

—HARVEY PENICK

Golf is the Great Mystery.

—P. G. WODEHOUSE

What separates the great players from the good players or the 15-handicap player from the 20-handicap player is not so much ability as brainpower and emotional equilibrium.

—ARNOLD PALMER

Golf is good for the soul. You get so mad at yourself you forget to hate your enemies.

—WILL ROGERS

Every day you don't hit balls is one day longer it takes you to get better.

—BEN HOGAN

The chief reaction among amateurs to poor putting, it seems to me, is exasperation, combined with a sort of vague hope that, by some kind of mini-miracle, it will all have gotten better by the next time they play.

—JACK NICKLAUS

I never did see the sense in keeping my head down. The only reason I play golf is to see where the ball goes.

—CHARLES PRICE

Why am I using a new putter? Because the old one didn't float too well.

—CRAIG SANDLER

You will hit the ball farther more frequently when you don't try to hit it far.

—SAM SNEAD

Ambition is a grievous fault...and grievously doth the duffer pay.

—WILLIAM SHAKESPEARE

In baseball, you can hit your home run over the right-field or center-field fence. In golf, everything has to be right over second base.

—KEN HARRELSON

Golf is the most overtaught and least-learned human endeavor. If they taught sex the way they teach golf, the race would have died out years ago.

—JIM MURRAY

I'd give up golf if I didn't have so many sweaters.

—BOB HOPE

Golf is a plague invented by Calvinist Scots as a punishment for man's sins.

—JAMES RESTON

Driving Yourself Insane

I lost only two golf balls last season—I was putting at the time.

In an amateur golf tournament, a player was carefully lining up his putt when a ball whizzed past his ear and landed on the green. After the foursome putted out, the golfer who had made the unnerving approach hurried up to his near-victim.

"Gosh, I'm sorry," he said. "I would have yelled 'Fore!' but I didn't want to ruin your putt."

—GLORIA BARSOCCHINI

Did you hear about the local country club that was determined to be politically correct? Instead of saying the golfers have handicaps, they say they're "stroke challenged."

Isn't it great to get out on the old golf course again and lie in the sun?

One statistician says there are more than 320 kinds of games played with balls. We, personally, have seen more than 320 kinds of games played with golf balls.

A flying saucer's mechanism went out of joint, and it came careening into a deep sand trap on the golf course. "What do I do now?" the pilot shortwaved to headquarters in outer space.

Back came the answer, "Use your number nine iron, you meathead!"

Q: Where do golfers dance?
A: At the golf ball.

A story was told about a choleric golfer who would fly into a rage every time he played. He finally hit upon the device of playing without a ball. This made him very happy.

A clubmate decided he'd play without a ball, too, and the two of them had a match every Saturday, complete with everything but balls!

One day they made a $100 bet on a round and the club members gathered to watch this most unusual match. The two players were all even as they hit off the eighteenth tee. Both had good drives, and they sauntered down the fairway to where a good drive would have landed.

The first player took a club and swung. Immediately, the other player started to yell at him, and in a moment there was a big fight. Club members rushed down from the eighteenth green to see what was wrong.

"It's my match! It's my match!" cried the second player. "He hit the wrong ball!"

With the way I play golf, the greens flags should be at half-mast.

The golfer was brought into the hospital suffering from sunstroke. The nurse began to read his temperature. "102-103-104—"

"Hey, Doc," whispered the suffering sport. "What's par for this hospital?"

Small girl, as golfer in sand trap pauses for breath: "He's stopped beating it, Mummy. I think it must be dead."

A North Carolina state booklet says: "Famous midsouth resorts, including Pinehurst and Southern Pines, have...more golf curses per mile than anywhere else in the world."

There's a tricky three-par hole on the golf course at Pebble Beach, California, that occasionally drives even the experts to distraction. A tongue of the Pacific Ocean surges in between the tee and the green, and only a well-directed two-hundred-yard drive can keep a player out of serious trouble.

Almost as disastrous as a drive into the briny sea is a hook shot onto the beach below the green. Bing Crosby found his ball there one windy day, and wasted seven shots trying to lift it up onto the green. The eighth try almost made it, but then began rolling back, picked up speed, and hit Bing in the stomach.

Crosby tossed his wedge to the caddie and said, "That settles it, son. When your ball starts to hit back at you, it's time to quit!"

My golf is improving. Yesterday I hit the ball in one.

A golf pro was teaching a new pupil how to swing his club. "Now that you have the right idea," the pro said, "just go through the motions without hitting the ball."

"I can already do that," the pupil said. "I want you to teach me how to hit it."

First golfer: Why do you play so much golf?
Second golfer: My doctor said I must take my iron every day.

I did as the pro told me. I kept my head down and my eyes on the ball. But wouldn't you know it? Some darned fool stole my cart.

I used to play golf, but then I lost my ball. The string broke.

There are 20 million golfers and only 19,999,999 balls, and that is why, at any given moment, someone is out looking for a lost golf ball.

An Oklahoma oil tycoon appeared at the local golf links to make a fourth. He was followed by a servant pulling an adjustable, foam-cushioned chaise longue behind him.

"Are you going to make that poor caddie lug that couch all over the course after you?" a fellow player asked.

"Caddie, my eye," explained the oil man. "That's my psychiatrist."

The golf nut approached Lyndon Johnson at the Democratic dinner and naturally tried to bring up his favorite subject. "What's your golf handicap, Mr. President?" he asked.

"I don't have any," the President answered. "I'm all handicap."

I've got more ways to slice than a delicatessen counterman!

I got a hole in one the other day, but I'm going crazy trying to figure out how to mount it!

First golfer: Did you read recently how a golfer got 912 holes out of a single golf ball?

Second golfer: Yes, I only got 36 holes out of the same brand of ball.

First golfer: Well, considering your game, yours is the stronger testimonial!

You should worry about playing with a guy who writes down his score and then wipes his fingerprints from the pencil.

Irate golfer: You must take your children away from here, madam. This is no place for them.

Mother: Don't you worry—they can't hear nothing new. Their father was a sergeant-major.

Then there's the Scot who gave up golf after 20 years. He lost his ball.

Golf is like children. It takes time and patience to master them.